This book is officially licensed by Winning Moves UK Ltd, owners of the Top Trumps registered trademark.

BBC, DOCTOR WHO (word marks, logos and devices), TARDIS, DALEKS, CYBERMAN and K-9 (word marks and devices) are trade marks of the British Broadcasting Corporation and are used under licence.

BBC logo © BBC 1996. Doctor Who logo © BBC 2004. TARDIS image © BBC 1963. Dalek image © BBC/Terry Nation 1963. Cyberman image © BBC/Kit Pedler/Gerry Davis 1966. K-9 image © BBC/Bob Baker/Dave Martin 1977.

The Daleks were created by Terry Nation.
The Cyberman was created by Kit Pedler and Gerry Davis.
K-9 was created by Bob Baker and Dave Martin.
Licensed by BBC Worldwide Limited.

Moray Laing has asserted his right to be identified as the author of this book.

British Library Cataloguing-in-Publication Data.
A catalogue record for this book is available from the British Library

ISBN 978 1 84425 643 3

Library of Congress catalog card no. 2008929394

Published by Haynes Publishing, Sparkford, Yeovil, Somerset BA22 7JJ, UK
Tel: +44 (0)1963 442030 Fax: +44 (0)1963 440001
Email: sales@haynes.co.uk Website: www.haynes.co.uk

Haynes North America Inc., 861 Lawrence Drive, Newbury Park, California 91320, USA

Printed and bound in Great Britain by J. H. Haynes & Co. Ltd, Sparkford

The Author

Moray Laing is the Editor of *Doctor Who Adventures* magazine. Like the Doctor, he knows a lot about monsters and time travel. He has written several books on the subject, including two other *Top Trumps Doctor Who* books.

TOP TRUMPS®

DOCTOR · WHO

Series Four

Contents

About
Top Trumps

It's now more than 30 years since Britain's kids first caught the Top Trumps craze. The game remained hugely popular until the 1990s, when it slowly drifted into obscurity. Then, in 1999, UK games company Winning Moves discovered it, bought it, dusted it down, gave it a thorough makeover and introduced it to a whole new generation. And so the Top Trumps legend continues.

Nowadays, there are Top Trumps titles for just about everyone, with subjects about animals, cars, ships, aircraft and all the great films and TV shows. Top Trumps is now even more popular than before. In Britain, a pack of Top Trumps is bought every six seconds! And it's not just British children who love the game. Children in Australasia, the Far East, the Middle East, all over Europe and in North America can buy Top Trumps at their local shops.

Today you can even play the game on the internet, interactive DVD, your games console and even your mobile phone.

You've played the game...

Now read the book!

Haynes Publishing and Top Trumps have teamed up to bring you this exciting new Top Trumps book, in which you will find even more pictures, details and statistics.

Top Trumps: Doctor Who features 45 key characters from the fourth series of the hugely successful television show, from Donna, Martha and Rose to Sontarans, Ood, Hath and, of course, Davros. Packed with stunning pictures, fascinating facts and all the vital statistics, this is the essential pocket guide.

Look out for other Top Trumps books from Haynes Publishing – even more facts, even more fun!

Donna Noble
Temp turned time traveller

Donna Noble meets the Doctor for the first time on her wedding day, when she finds herself at the centre of an alien plot to awaken millions of hibernating Racnoss. Later she starts to regret turning down the Doctor's offer to travel in the TARDIS so she spends a year trying to find him. They run into each other when they are both investigating Adipose Industries, and this time Donna decides to join the Doctor for adventures in time and space. Life with the Time Lord is very different from her life as an office temp. She sees so many amazing things and even saves the entire universe from destruction. However, when she touches the Doctor's spare hand she becomes part Time Lord and this nearly kills her. To save his friend, the Doctor returns her home and wipes her mind of all memories of monsters, the TARDIS and her time with him.

Statistics

DEBUT	*The Runaway Bride* (2006)
PLAYED BY	Catherine Tate
HOME	London, England
STATUS	Friend
HEIGHT	1.73m
SCARE RATING	[2] Harmless, but has a quick temper
SPECIAL FEATURES	[9] Becomes part Time Lord, 100 words per minute
WEAPONS	[1] Not applicable
LIKES	The Doctor, speaking her mind, her granddad
DISLIKES	Her old life as a temp, being bossed around
TALK	'I don't know what sort of kids you've been flying around with in outer space but you're not telling me to shut up!'

Bannakaffalatta

Spiky-faced cyborg

Bannakaffalatta is a small spiky-faced cyborg that is travelling aboard the luxury cruise liner called the Titanic. Some time ago he was involved in an accident, and he had to have parts of his body replaced. He is ashamed of being a cyborg, though, and wants to keep it secret. He meets the Doctor when they teleport to Earth on Christmas Eve along with a small group of fellow passengers and a waitress called Astrid. When meteors hit the Titanic, he teams up with the Doctor to help save the ship from destruction. The Doctor asks Bannakaffalatta if he can call him Banna, but he doesn't let him. Using an electromagnetic pulse from his EMP transmitter to destroy some Host, the brave cyborg gives his life to help save others.

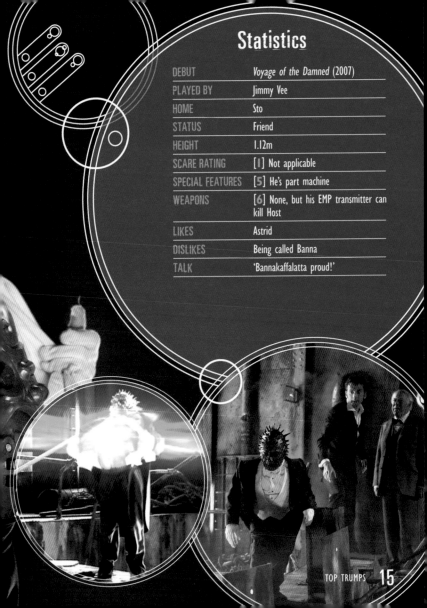

Statistics

DEBUT	*Voyage of the Damned* (2007)
PLAYED BY	Jimmy Vee
HOME	Sto
STATUS	Friend
HEIGHT	1.12m
SCARE RATING	[1] Not applicable
SPECIAL FEATURES	[5] He's part machine
WEAPONS	[6] None, but his EMP transmitter can kill Host
LIKES	Astrid
DISLIKES	Being called Banna
TALK	'Bannakaffalatta proud!'

Astrid Peth

Waitress turned adventurer

Astrid Peth is from the planet Sto in the Cassavalian Belt. She dreams of seeing other worlds and she works in a spaceport diner for three years before getting a job as a waitress aboard the Titanic. The crew on the cruise liner are not allowed to leave the ship but the Doctor uses his psychic paper to convince Mr Copper that Astrid and him are signed up for a short trip to Earth in the teleport. She thinks it is amazing. When the Titanic runs into trouble, Astrid helps the Doctor save the ship. She asks if she can travel in the TARDIS with the Doctor – and he immediately says yes. But when she discovers that her boss, Max Capricorn, is sabotaging the ship she stops him with a forklift truck and they both fall into the damaged ship's engines. The Doctor uses the ship's teleport to recall her suspended molecules, but he is too late to save her.

Statistics

DEBUT	*Voyage of the Damned* (2007)
PLAYED BY	Kylie Minogue
HOME	Sto
STATUS	Friend
HEIGHT	1.53m
SCARE RATING	[1] Not applicable
SPECIAL FEATURES	[7] Helpful waitress, good in a crisis
WEAPONS	[6] Uses an EMP transmitter to kill Host
LIKES	The Doctor, dreaming of other worlds
DISLIKES	Being stuck on ship, waiting on tables
TALK	'Alien shops! Real alien shops! Look, you can't see the stars! And it smells, it stinks, this is amazing. Thank you!'

Max Capricorn
Corrupt businessman

Max Capricorn is the President of
a fleet of intergalactic cruise liners.
Max is just a severed head on top
of a life-support machine on wheels
and because cyborgs are hated in
his part of the galaxy, Max runs the
company as a hologram and poses
as an ordinary humanoid. When his
company turns on him because the
business is failing, Max comes up with
a plan to get his revenge. He uses
robots called Heavenly Host to kill
most of the crew and passengers on
one of his cruise liners – the Titanic
– and makes the ship's captain lower
the shields. He plans to lock himself
inside an indestructible Omnistate
Impact Chamber and let the Titanic
crash to Earth. He wants to retire
to the beaches of Penhaxico Two
– while the board of Max Capricorn
Cruise liners is put in jail for
destroying an entire planet. He is
killed when Astrid Peth pushes him
into the engines of the Titanic.

Statistics

DEBUT	*Voyage of the Damned* (2007)
PLAYED BY	George Costigan
HOME	Sto
STATUS	Bad loser enemy
HEIGHT	1.5m
SCARE RATING	[7] Shocking sight
SPECIAL FEATURES	[6] A gold tooth, a glass eye
WEAPONS	[6] Heavenly Host
LIKES	Winning, money, bribery
DISLIKES	Losing
TALK	'I never lose.'

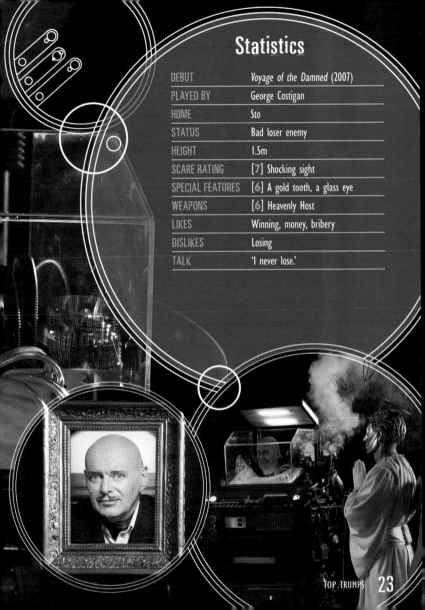

Heavenly Host

Robotic angels

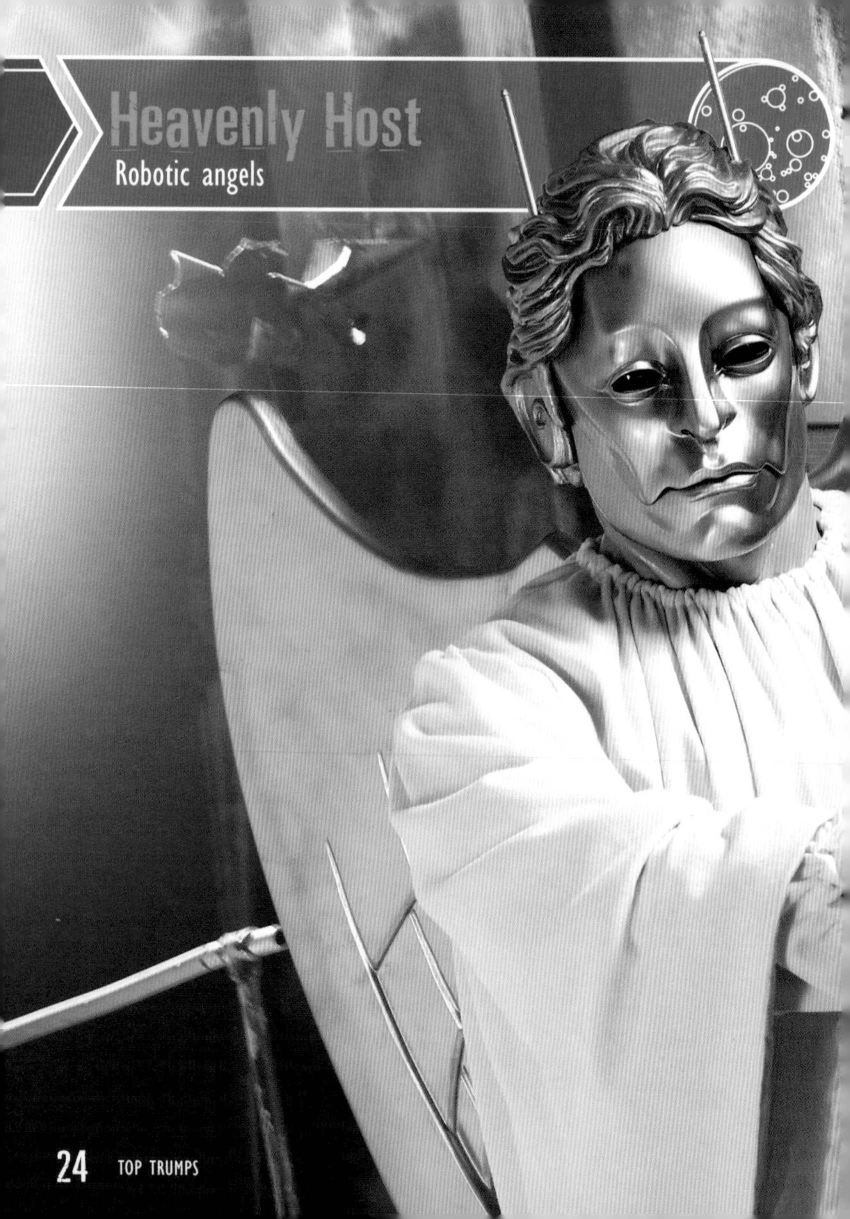

Heavenly Host
Robotic angels

Heavenly Host may look like beautiful golden angels, but they are certainly not angelic. These powerful robots all look the same, with blank, expressionless faces, complete with wings and haloes. Positioned throughout the Titanic cruise liner, the Host's primary purpose is to give tourist information to passengers. When the Host start to malfunction, engineers aboard the ship are surprised when the robots attack them, using their golden haloes as deadly weapons. The Host are part of Max Capricorn's plan to crash the Titanic into Earth and they are programmed to kill the passengers and crew ensuring that no one survives. The Heavenly Host attack the Doctor, Astrid and their friends, but Astrid is able to destroy some of them with Bannakaffalatta's EMP transmitter. The Host are also able to fly, and they carry the Doctor to the bridge. When Max dies, the Host revert to the next highest authority – and that's the Doctor!

Statistics

DEBUT	*Voyage of the Damned* (2007)
PLAYED BY	Various
HOME	Built on Sto
STATUS	Enemy robots
HEIGHT	1.95m
SCARE RATING	[8] Horrible haloes
SPECIAL FEATURES	[7] Can fly, angelic faces
WEAPONS	[7] Haloes
LIKES	Max Capricorn, obeying orders, destruction
DISLIKES	EMP transmitters
TALK	'Information: kill.'

Morvin and Foon Van Hoff are a married couple from the planet Sto. They work in a Milk Market and are good at repairing robots because they work with robot staff. Foon wins tickets for a trip on the Titanic in a competition by naming all five husbands of Joofie Crystalle in a television programme called *By The Light of the Asteroid*. However, Foon spent five thousand credits phoning the competition vone line – much more than the value of the prize. On Christmas Eve they dress as a cowboy and cowgirl because a group of passengers think it is funny to tell them it is a fancy dress evening. Morvin falls into the Titanic engines by accident and later his wife sacrifices herself by using the lasso from her cowgirl costume to pull a Host into the engines with her.

Statistics

DEBUT	*Voyage of the Damned* (2007)
PLAYED BY	Clive Rowe (Morvin) and Debbie Chazen (Foon)
HOME	Sto
STATUS	Unlucky winners
HEIGHT	Morvin is 1.78m and Foon is 1.52m
SCARE RATING	[1] Not applicable
SPECIAL FEATURES	[5] Good with robots
WEAPONS	[1] Not applicable, but Foon uses her lasso
LIKES	Each other, eating, *By The Light of the Asteroid*
DISLIKES	Host, annoying passengers
TALK	Foon: 'Have a buffalo wing! They must be huge, these buffalo, so many wings!'

Wilfred Mott

Donna's granddad

Wilfred Mott
Donna's granddad

Wilf Mott is Donna's granddad. He lives with Donna and his daughter Sylvia in Chiswick in London. Wilf meets the Doctor for the first time when the Time Lord teleports to Earth from the Titanic. Wilf is one of the few people to stay behind in London at Christmas because of recent invasions – and he is selling newspapers on an unusually quiet Christmas Eve. When Donna tells him she is looking for a man in a blue box, Wilf is concerned for his granddaughter, and doesn't realise she is talking about someone he has already met. His favourite hobby is sitting in his allotment looking at the stars with his telescope. For a while, Wilf is the only person that knows Donna is travelling in time and space with an alien – and when the Doctor wipes the Doctor's mind, he is forced to keep her travels in the TARDIS secret forever.

Statistics

DEBUT	*Voyage of the Damned* (2007)
PLAYED BY	Bernard Cribbins
HOME	London, England
STATUS	Friend
HEIGHT	1.78m
SCARE RATING	[1] Not applicable
SPECIAL FEATURES	[5] Knows about stars
WEAPONS	[1] Not applicable — although he attacks a Dalek with a paint gun
LIKES	Astronomy, Donna
DISLIKES	Aliens
TALK	'Every night, Doctor. When it goes dark. And the stars come out. I'll look up. On her behalf. I'll look up at the sky and think of you.'

Sylvia Noble
Donna's mum

Sylvia Noble
Donna's mum

Sylvia Noble is Donna's mum. She can be quite bossy and unsupportive of her daughter at times, but Donna is usually able to ignore this or fight back if she has to! Sylvia doesn't want Donna to work at H.C. Clements but, luckily, Donna doesn't listen to her mother's advice. If she had, she would have never met the Doctor. Sylvia thinks Donna is seeking attention when she disappears on her wedding day, not realising the danger Donna is facing until she witnesses robots destroy the wedding reception. For a long time, Sylvia doesn't know that Donna is travelling in time and space with a Time Lord. It is only when she meets Rose Tyler that Sylvia finally becomes aware of how important Donna is, discovering that her daughter is the key to saving the entire universe. Sylvia is angry when the Doctor insults her relationship with her daughter, although she now has the chance to change this.

Statistics

DEBUT	*The Runaway Bride* (2006)
PLAYED BY	Jacqueline King
HOME	London, England
STATUS	Friend
HEIGHT	1.76m
SCARE RATING	[1] Not applicable
SPECIAL FEATURES	[2] Likes to moan at Donna, good with an axe
WEAPONS	[1] Not applicable
LIKES	Her family, her home
DISLIKES	Daleks, the Doctor
TALK	'It's no good sitting there dreaming, no one's gonna come along with a magic wand and make your life all better.'

Matron Cofelia
Nasty nanny

Matron Cofelia
Nasty nanny

Matron Cofelia is the real name of an intergalactic nanny. On Earth, she sets up a company called Adipose Industries and calls herself Miss Foster. She claims that a small diet pill will help the population lose weight – but it is part of an alien plan to breed new creatures from human fat. Matron Cofelia is part of the Five-Straighten Classabindi Nursery Fleet, Intergalactic Class, and is employed by the Adiposian First Family. Her role is to help create a new generation of Adipose creatures after the Family's breeding planet mysteriously disappears. She takes her work incredibly seriously, and won't let anyone get in her way. What she is doing on Earth is against Galactic Law and potentially dangerous to humans. When the Adiposian First Family arrive to collect the new babies, they let Matron Cofelia fall to her death to remove evidence of their crime.

Statistics

DEBUT	*Partners in Crime* (2008)
PLAYED BY	Sarah Lancashire
HOME	Five-Straighten Classabindi Nursery Fleet
STATUS	Nasty nanny
HEIGHT	1.73m
SCARE RATING	[7] Mean and focussed
SPECIAL FEATURES	[5] Glasses, running a profitable business
WEAPONS	[6] Sonic pen
LIKES	Adipose babies
DISLIKES	The Doctor, being questioned
TALK	'One capsule, once a day, for three weeks. And the fat, as they say, just walks away.'

Adipose
Little fat monsters

Adipose
Little fat monsters

Adipose are creatures from the planet Adipose Three, and they are made from living fat. Their children are incredibly small with dark shiny eyes and one single tooth. They like to smile and wave and look quite sweet. When the breeding planet disappears, the Adipose are forced to find a way for their race to continue, so they employ Matron Cofelia to help. She distributes Adipose seeds inside diet pills that, when swallowed, attract all the fat cells inside a human body to form a baby Adipose. The process is meant to be harmless, although distressing for the carrier. In an emergency the Adipose can use an entire body to create a number of new Adipose, although this isn't good for them and results in the host body being completely destroyed. The Adiposian First Family eventually come to Earth to collect the newly born Adipose and kill Matron Cofelia.

Statistics

DEBUT	*Partners in Crime* (2008)
PLAYED BY	Computer generated
HOME	Adipose Three
STATUS	Cute aliens
HEIGHT	0.15m when born
SCARE RATING	[2] More of a shock than a scare
SPECIAL FEATURES	[2] One little tooth, bright eyes
WEAPONS	[1] Not applicable
LIKES	Fat, smiling
DISLIKES	Consuming whole bodies
TALK	'Mew!'

Sibylline Sisterhood

Soothsaying sisters

Sibylline Sisterhood

Soothsaying sisters

The Sibylline Sisterhood is a group of female soothsayers from Pompeii. Led by a High Priestess, the Sisters worship in the Temple of Sibyl in the heart of the town. Like many others in Pompeii, the Sisters have the power of predicting the future – extremely accurately. Breathing in the dust and vapours from Vesuvius is slowly turning people into stone and giving them special powers. The Sisters are also able to communicate with each other telepathically. In the Thirteenth Book of the Sibylline Oracles there is mention of a blue box arriving in Pompeii – the TARDIS. The Sybil said that the box would appear at the time of storms and fire and betrayal. The High Priestess of the Sibylline Sisterhood is changing into an alien called a Pyrovile, and these aliens prevent the Sisterhood from seeing the destruction of Pompeii.

Statistics

DEBUT	*The Fires of Pompeii* (2008)
PLAYED BY	Sasha Behar (Spurrina), Lorraine Burroughs (Thalina), Karen Gillan (Soothsayer), Victoria Wicks (High Priestess)
HOME	Pompeii
STATUS	Spooky sisterhood
HEIGHT	Various
SCARE RATING	[3] They try to kill Donna
SPECIAL FEATURES	[3] They have eye symbols on the backs of their hands
WEAPONS	[3] Daggers
LIKES	Predicting, worshipping Sibyl
DISLIKES	Men in their temple
TALK	'Words of wisdom, words of power!'

Pyroviles
Sinister stone creatures

Pyroviles
Sinister stone creatures

Pyroviles are rock-based creatures from Pyrovillia. When their home planet goes missing, a group of Pyroviles manage to escape but crash into Earth near the site of what becomes the town of Pompeii. They fall so quickly that the stone monsters smash to pieces and become dust. For thousands of years they are forgotten about until Vesuvius becomes active and wakes them up. The Pyroviles use the power from Vesuvius to convert people into stone and, as the people of Pompeii breath in the alien dust particles, they slowly start to change. The High Priestess of the Sibylline is at the halfway stage, but the people of Pompeii will soon turn into adult Pyroviles – massive monsters that want to turn Earth into a new Pyrovillia. They are destroyed when the Doctor and Donna blow up the alien energy converter, causing Mount Vesuvius to erupt. Twenty thousand people in Pompeii die as a result, but the world is saved.

Statistics

DEBUT	*The Fires of Pompeii* (2008)
PLAYED BY	Computer generated
HOME	Pyrovillia
STATUS	Rock monsters
HEIGHT	Adult Pyroviles up to 3m
SCARE RATING	[8] Keep back from the flames!
SPECIAL FEATURES	[7] The ability to convert people into creatures like them
WEAPONS	[7] Fire
LIKES	Fire, roaring, hot places
DISLIKES	Water pistols
TALK	'The breath of a Pyrovile will incinerate you, Doctor!'

Ood
Servant race

Ood are a race of telepathic servant creatures in the 42nd century that can be found on many planets across the Second Great and Bountiful Human Empire. Natural Ood used to roam on the ice plains of their home planet, the Ood-Sphere in the Horsehead Nebula. A company called Ood Operations breed Ood and convert the creatures into a race that can be sold to other worlds. The Ood have their hindbrain cut off and have a translator ball put in its place. In this way, a workforce of Ood that is ready to serve and communicate is created. The Ood are easily taken over by creatures with more powerful minds – and when they do, their eyes turn red, which signifies infection. A group called FOTO, which stands for Friends of the Ood, thinks Ood shouldn't be sold as 'slaves' – and fights for their freedom.

Statistics

DEBUT	*The Impossible Planet* (2006)
PLAYED BY	Various. Voiced by Silas Carson
HOME	Ood-Sphere in the Horsehead Nebula
STATUS	Unwilling servants
HEIGHT	1.83m
SCARE RATING	[7] Look out for red eyes!
SPECIAL FEATURES	[7] Can communicate telepathically
WEAPONS	[7] Their translator ball can electrocute
LIKES	Freedom
DISLIKES	Being treated as slaves
TALK	'The circle must be broken.'

Klineman Halpen
Chief Executive of Ood Operations

Klineman Halpen is the ruthless Chief Executive of Ood Operations. Converting Ood into servants that can be sold across the galaxy is a family business. Halpen's father showed him the warehouse containing the Ood Brain when he was very young – and he always knew the chilling truth about the Ood conversion. When sales of Ood begin to slow down, Halpen wants to reduce the price but double the amount of Ood that are converted. Halpen arrives on the Ood-Sphere after the Ood Management discover that some of the Ood are infected and are killing people. He is losing his hair and is drinking what he thinks is a hair tonic to help it grow back. What he doesn't realise it that his faithful servant, Ood Sigma, is giving him a special drink that eventually turns him into Oodkind.

Statistics

DEBUT	*Planet of the Ood* (2008)
PLAYED BY	Tim McInnerny
HOME	Unknown
STATUS	Bullying businessman
HEIGHT	1.85m
SCARE RATING	[3] Fierce anger
SPECIAL FEATURES	[5] Balding, becomes Oodkind
WEAPONS	[1] Not applicable
LIKES	Money
DISLIKES	The Ood Brain
TALK	'We're exporting hundreds of thousands of Ood, to all civilised planets... If they all turn rabid, you what it'll mean?'

Ood Brain
Ood telepathic centre

The Ood Brain is a massive pulsating brain and it is very important to Oodkind. The brain allows the Ood to communicate with each other through the most beautiful songs. Oodkind needs the Brain to survive – and if it dies, the Ood would die too. An Ood is unable to survive with only its forebrain and hindbrain because without the vital third shared Brain, they would constantly be at war with themselves. Long before Ood Operations starts processing Ood, the Ood Brain was found beneath the Northern Glacier on the Ood-Sphere. It was captured and locked up in a warehouse, where a telepathic barrier was put around it to stop the Ood communicating with it. Dr Ryder, who is a Friends of the Ood activist, gets into Ood Operations and lowers the strength of the barrier that is enslaving the brain – allowing the Ood to fight back.

Statistics

DEBUT	*Planet of the Ood* (2008)
PLAYED BY	Computer generated
HOME	Ood-Sphere in the Horsehead Nebula
STATUS	Big brain
HEIGHT	Massive
SCARE RATING	[7] Shock factor
SPECIAL FEATURES	[7] Telepathic when allowed to communicate
WEAPONS	[1] Not applicable
LIKES	Singing, all Oodkind
DISLIKES	Being held captive
TALK	Not applicable

Dr Martha Jones
Faithful friend

When she first meets the Doctor, Martha Jones is training to be a doctor herself. She loves travelling with the Doctor in the TARDIS very much, but after the Master almost destroys the human race and enslaves her family, she decides to stay behind on Earth. By this stage, she also realises that the Doctor hasn't noticed how much she cares for him – so thinks it is best to stop travelling with him. Martha leaves her mobile phone with him so that she can call him if she needs him. Back on Earth, Martha gets engaged to Tom Milligan – a doctor who travels the world – and she now works for the Unified Intelligence Taskforce, known as UNIT. She calls the Doctor on her old phone to bring the Time Lord back to Earth to help with a suspected alien attack. She is eventually promoted to Medical Director of UNIT and helps save Earth from a Dalek invasion.

Statistics

DEBUT	*Smith and Jones* (2007)
PLAYED BY	Freema Agyeman
HOME	London
STATUS	Friend
HEIGHT	1.53n
SCARE RATING	[1] Not applicable
SPECIAL FEATURES	[9] Medical Director
WEAPONS	[1] Not applicable, although she is going to use the Osterhagen Key to blow up Earth
LIKES	The Doctor, Tom Milligan, helping others
DISLIKES	Injustice
TALK	'You know the Doctor, he's wonderful, he's brilliant, but... he's like fire. Stand too close and people get burnt.'

Luke Rattigan
Child genius

Luke Rattigan is a child genius who helps the Sontaran race in a mission to take over Earth. When Luke Rattigan was 12 years old, he invented the Fountain Six Search Engine and became a millionaire overnight. Later he set up the Rattigan Academy, a private school that educates other genius children from all over the world. Along with his new alien friends, he is the mastermind behind ATMOS (Atmospheric Omission System), a revolutionary new device that reduces harmful CO_2 emissions down to zero. The device is fitted to cars across the planet, turning the vehicles into millions of weapons. Luke discovers that the Sontarans are not really interested in his survival, and merely using him to help advance their plans. To save the Doctor and Earth, Luke teleports aboard the Sontaran ship and blows it up, killing himself in the process.

Statistics

DEBUT	*The Sontaran Stratagem* (2008)
PLAYED BY	Ryan Sampson
HOME	Just outside London, England
STATUS	Traitor
HEIGHT	1.63m
SCARE RATING	[4] Powerful, spoiled and slightly mad
SPECIAL FEATURES	[6] Genius
WEAPONS	[5] His brain
LIKES	Winning, succeeding, being right
DISLIKES	The Doctor
TALK	'I think that makes my answer clear, don't you?'

Sontarans are short creatures from the planet Sontar and are the finest warriors in the galaxy. They might look incredibly small, but they are very dangerous and love war. The Sontarans are a race of clones so all look identical and are very difficult to tell apart. They are grown in batches of millions and only have one real weakness – their Probic Vent. This hole in the back of their neck is used for feeding and if you hit the Probic Vent a Sontaran will collapse in agony. The Sontarans have been locked in battle with their oldest enemies, the Rutans, for thousands of years. A group of Sontarans use Luke Rattigan to develop ATMOS. They plan to release gas from inside the ATMOS device into the atmosphere, killing everyone on Earth, and turn the planet into a new clone world – but the Doctor stops them with the help of Luke.

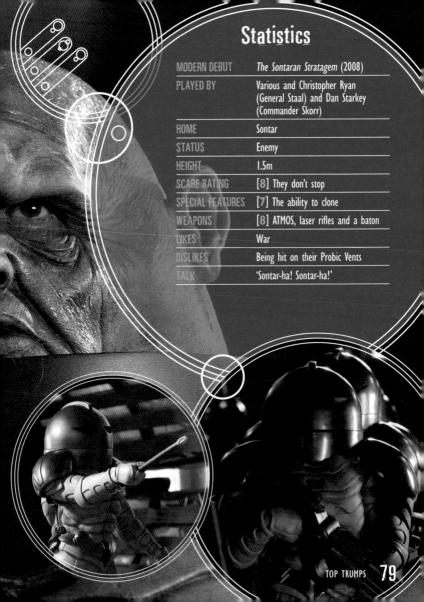

Statistics

MODERN DEBUT	*The Sontaran Stratagem* (2008)
PLAYED BY	Various and Christopher Ryan (General Staal) and Dan Starkey (Commander Skorr)
HOME	Sontar
STATUS	Enemy
HEIGHT	1.5m
SCARE RATING	[8] They don't stop
SPECIAL FEATURES	[7] The ability to clone
WEAPONS	[8] ATMOS, laser rifles and a baton
LIKES	War
DISLIKES	Being hit on their Probic Vents
TALK	'Sontar-ha! Sontar-ha!'

Jenny
The Doctor's daughter

Jenny
The Doctor's daughter

Jenny is born on the planet Messaline when a tissue sample is taken from the Doctor's hand and put into a Progenation Machine. It produces a young woman with many of the Doctor's traits – and also many he doesn't have. She's born to join the fight against creatures called the Hath. She has an instant mental download of all strategic and military protocols – a Generation 5000 Soldier at Combat Level ready to take on the Hath. The Doctor calls her a 'generated anomaly', and Donna decides that sounds like Jenny, so the name stays. The Doctor offers Jenny the chance to travel with him, but she is shot while saving her dad. The Doctor leaves, thinking she is dead, but the power of the terraforming planet brings her back to life. Jenny steals a spaceship and flies off to explore the universe.

Statistics

DEBUT	*The Doctor's Daughter* (2008)
PLAYED BY	Georgia Moffett
HOME	Messaline
STATUS	Friend
HEIGHT	1.57m
SCARE RATING	[1] Not applicable
SPECIAL FEATURES	[8] Clever, just like her dad
WEAPONS	[7] Guns
LIKES	Fighting, her dad
DISLIKES	Being told what to do
TALK	'I'm not a monkey. Or a child.'

Hath
Bubbling creatures

The Hath are fish-faced creatures on the planet Messaline. They communicate in bubbles, and have a water-filled tube where you would expect to find their mouth. One Hath, called Peck, becomes friends with Martha after kidnapping her. She uses her medical knowledge to help Peck when he hurts himself. Strangely, the TARDIS isn't able to translate the bubbling language, so Martha has to guess what her new friend is saying. The Hath on Messaline have been at war with the humans there for generations – even though the war lasts just seven days. The Hath and humans are meant to be colonising a new world together, but break into two separate groups and end up using Progenation Machines to build new generations of their race to fight at an alarming rate. When the barren planet of Messaline is transformed into a beautiful lush planet, the war ends and humans and Hath live together again.

Statistics

DEBUT	*The Doctor's Daughter* (2008)
PLAYED BY	Various and Ruari Mears (Gable) and Paul Casey (Peck)
HOME	Messaline
STATUS	Warring creatures
HEIGHT	Various
SCARE RATING	[3] Fierce looking fish
SPECIAL FEATURES	[3] A bubbling tube on their faces
WEAPONS	[3] Guns
LIKES	Fighting
DISLIKES	Humans
TALK	'Bubble, bubble, bubble, gurgle.'

Vespiform
Insect race

The Vespiform are a race of insect creatures with hives in the Silfrax galaxy. They look like giant wasps and possess a powerful sting in their tale, just like the wasps they resemble – but this sting is much more powerful and dangerous. The Vespiform are able to transform into other species to disguise and protect themselves. One creature does this in the late 19th century and falls in love with a human called Lady Eddison. She has the alien's child, and the boy doesn't realise he is part-Vespiform until many years later. The child grows up to become the Reverend Arnold Golightly. When thieves break into his church his anger breaks the genetic lock – and the vicar turns into a giant wasp. A Vespiform Telepathic Recorder, which Lady Eddison thinks is a necklace, beams his alien identity into him and he absorbs the works of Agatha Christie at the same time.

Statistics

DEBUT	*The Unicorn and the Wasp* (2008)
PLAYED BY	Computer generated and Tom Goodman-Hill (as Reverend Golightly)
HOME	Silfrax galaxy
STATUS	Vicious alien
HEIGHT	2.95m
SCARE RATING	[8] Especially if you don't like wasps
SPECIAL FEATURES	[8] Ability to transform into other species
WEAPONS	[7] A sting
LIKES	Buzzing and stinging
DISLIKES	Water
TALK	'Bzzzzzzzzzzzzz.'

Agatha Christie
Crime writer

Agatha Christie is the best-selling crime novelist of all time. She is a clever woman who loves a mystery, but she doesn't think that her writing is very good. However, she will go on to be loved as a writer for millions of years after her death – her books are still published in the year Five Billion. In 1926, Agatha goes missing for ten days and turns up in a hotel in Harrogate saying that she has lost her memory. Before that she is at a house party with Lady Eddison and the Doctor and Donna, where she becomes central to a series of murders caused by a Vespiform. The creature becomes connected to Agatha after absorbing her writing, but when it drowns in a lake, it releases her and wipes her memory – although traces of the strange events and characters can be found in her writing.

Statistics

DEBUT	*The Unicorn and the Wasp* (2008)
PLAYED BY	Fenella Woolgar
HOME	England
STATUS	The best crime writer!
HEIGHT	1.68m
SCARE RATING	[1] Not applicable
SPECIAL FEATURES	[8] A brilliant brain
WEAPONS	[8] Words
LIKES	Writing, mysteries,
DISLIKES	Fools, being talked about
TALK	'Every murder is essentially the same. They are committed because somebody wants something.'

Doctor Moon
Secret helper

A doctor moon is a virus-checking computer program. It is set up to support the main computer of the Library planet in the 51st century, inside an artificial moon placed in orbit around the planet. Inside the Library computer, it takes the form of a character called Doctor Moon, a gentle man with a calm voice who appears to be a psychologist. Doctor Moon looks after the young girl whose mind lives inside the computer. To save the Library, Doctor Moon upsets the girl by telling her that her real world is a lie and that her nightmares are actually real life – and that the people trapped inside the Library need her help. Donna meets Doctor Moon when she is saved inside the computer – he tells her that he has been treating her for two years. Donna is confused for a moment, and then believes him, as she becomes part of the strange world.

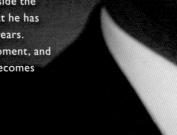

Statistics

DEBUT	*Silence in the Library* (2008)
PLAYED BY	Colin Salmon
HOME	The Library computer
STATUS	Virus checker
HEIGHT	1.93m
SCARE RATING	[1] Not applicable
SPECIAL FEATURES	[4] Calming
WEAPONS	[1] Not applicable
LIKES	Listening, helping, talking
DISLIKES	Danger in the Library
TALK	'The shadows are moving again. Those people are depending on you. Only you can save them!'

Professor River Song
Future friend

Professor River Song

Future friend

Professor River Song knows the Doctor very well – or at least she will do at some point in his future travels. River is part of a team that comes to explore a Library planet and find out what has happened to all the people that went missing. She sends a message to the Doctor on his psychic paper, but when she meets the Doctor and Donna she is surprised the Time Lord doesn't recognise her. She eventually realises that the Doctor hasn't met her yet and is only able to convince the Doctor that she is telling the truth by whispering his real name. She carries a diary that looks like the outside of the TARDIS and has a sonic screwdriver that the future Doctor has given her. She dies saving the Library, but the Doctor is able to save her to the main computer, where she is reunited with her old friends.

Statistics

DEBUT	*Silence in the Library* (2008)
PLAYED BY	Alex Kingston
HOME	Unknown
STATUS	Friend
HEIGHT	1.70m
SCARE RATING	[1] Not applicable
SPECIAL FEATURES	[8] Knows a lot about the Doctor's future
WEAPONS	[7] Squareness gun
LIKES	The Doctor, danger, excitement
DISLIKES	Spoiling what's going to happen
TALK	'Life with a time traveller — never knew it would be such hard work!'

Charlotte Abigail Lux

Mysterious girl

Charlotte Abigail Lux

Mysterious girl

Charlotte Abigail Lux is a young girl
who is dying. To protect her, her
father builds a vast Library world and
puts her living mind inside the main
computer, with the biggest hard drive
ever, in the centre of the planet. By
doing this he creates a virtual world
for his daughter to live in happily
and safely forever, giving her access
to every book ever written. It is her
father's decision that no one should
know that his daughter is here and
that she should be left in peace with
all the books, and she has a Doctor
Moon inside the computer to look
after her. But when the Vashta
Nerada attacks the Library, the
young girl saves all the people in the
Library by taking them out of reality
and saving them inside the computer,
leaving her with over 4,000 living
minds inside her head.

Statistics

DEBUT	*Silence in the Library* (2008)
PLAYED BY	Eve Newton
HOME	The Library computer
STATUS	Friend
HEIGHT	1.5m
SCARE RATING	[1] Not applicable
SPECIAL FEATURES	[9] She has a whole world around her and every book in existence
WEAPONS	[1] Not applicable
LIKES	Books, dreaming
DISLIKES	Vashta Nerada, being told what to do
TALK	'Something's here. Something's got in. No one's supposed to get in!'

Nodes are tall statues found throughout the Library and are used to access information from the main computer. On top of the statue is a life-size human face that revolves to look at the person it is addressing. When accessing information, a face is chosen based on what it thinks the Node user would like to see. A Node called Courtesy Node seven-one-zero-slash aqua gives the Doctor and Donna a message from the head librarian. It tells them that the Library has been sealed off and that if they want to live they must count the shadows. The Node faces are made up from the faces of all the people who are saved inside the Library computer. When Donna is saved to the computer hard drive, a Node with her face appears and tells the Doctor that Donna Noble has been saved and has left the Library.

Statistics

DEBUT	*Silence in the Library* (2008)
PLAYED BY	Various
HOME	The Library
STATUS	Scary statues
HEIGHT	2.5m
SCARE RATING	[3] Not scary — until you realise it's a dead person's face
SPECIAL FEATURES	[4] Can access a face it thinks you will like
WEAPONS	[1] Not applicable
LIKES	Giving information
DISLIKES	Being asked too many questions
TALK	'Donna Noble has been saved. Donna Noble has left the Library.'

Vashta Nerada

Scary shadows

Vashta Nerada

Scary shadows

Vashta Nerada are found in the dark and live in shadows. The Doctor calls them piranhas of the air. A Vashta Nerada can strip human flesh in seconds. The creatures live on all the worlds in the same planetary system as the Library and have led to people's fear of the dark. They hunt in forests and lay their spores in trees. However, millions of microspores end up in the Library when forests containing Vashta Nerada are pulped, printed and bound without realising and are turned into millions and million of books. When the Vashta Nerada reach their hatching cycle they start attacking the people in the Library. The main computer teleports everyone out of danger and saves them on the hard drive at the core of the planet. The Vashta Nerada give the Doctor a day to get everyone safely out of the Library before they hatch.

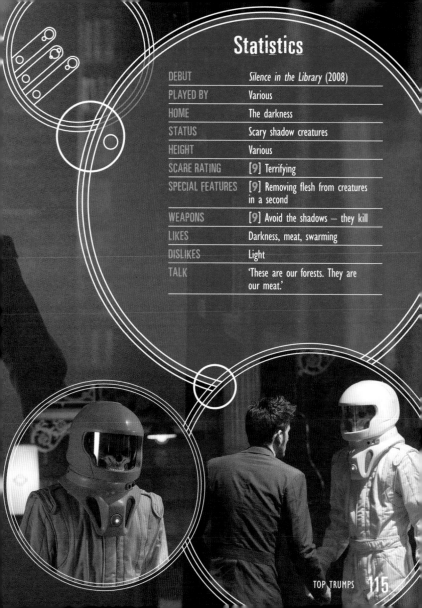

Statistics

DEBUT	*Silence in the Library* (2008)
PLAYED BY	Various
HOME	The darkness
STATUS	Scary shadow creatures
HEIGHT	Various
SCARE RATING	[9] Terrifying
SPECIAL FEATURES	[9] Removing flesh from creatures in a second
WEAPONS	[9] Avoid the shadows — they kill
LIKES	Darkness, meat, swarming
DISLIKES	Light
TALK	'These are our forests. They are our meat.'

Lee McAvoy
Donna's virtual husband

Lee McAvoy is in the Library when the Vashta Nerada attack. He has a bad stammer and becomes trapped inside the virtual world of Charlotte Abigail Lux, along with over 4,000 other people. Lee meets Donna when she is uploaded to the computer. They are both being treated by Doctor Moon inside the computer. They go on a fishing trip and then, seconds later, suddenly they discover they are married. In the virtual world they have twins called Ella and Joshua and seven years pass in a flash. Lee is disturbed by a letter Donna receives, telling her that the world is wrong. The letter is from Miss Evangelista who explains to Donna that her family is not real. As their virtual world falls apart, Donna promises to find Lee whatever happens. Lee spots Donna back in the Library, but his stammer prevents him from getting her attention and he is teleported off the world.

Statistics

DEBUT	*Forest of the Dead* (2008)
PLAYED BY	Jason Pitt
HOME	Unknown
STATUS	Donna's virtual husband
HEIGHT	1.85m
SCARE RATING	[1] Not applicable
SPECIAL FEATURES	[2] Caring
WEAPONS	[1] Not applicable
LIKES	Donna and his family, fishing
DISLIKES	His stammer
TALK	'Am I real?'

Sky Silvestry
Unfortunate businesswoman

Sky Silvestry is a businesswoman. She takes a trip aboard the Crusader 50 on the planet Midnight to see a beautiful sapphire waterfall. Other passengers on board include the Doctor, who Sky instantly likes as he seems to be the sanest person on the trip. When the Crusader 50 breaks down in the middle of nowhere, a mysterious presence starts banging on the side of the vehicle. Eventually, it feeds on Sky's fear and gets inside her head. Possessed by the alien, Sky starts to repeat everything that people are saying. As it gets stronger, Sky starts to say things at exactly the same time. The final stage involves people following Sky's words. When the Doctor starts to repeat Sky, the others on the Crusader decide to throw him outside – but the Hostess realises Sky is still possessed and sacrifices herself by pulling Sky and the alien force outside with her.

Statistics

DEBUT	*Midnight* (2008)
PLAYED BY	Lesley Sharp
HOME	Unknown
STATUS	Possessed woman
HEIGHT	1.82m
SCARE RATING	[9] Terrifying
SPECIAL FEATURES	[9] Can adapt and copy people
WEAPONS	[1] Unknown
LIKES	To copy
DISLIKES	The Doctor
TALK	'What are you looking at me for? It's not my fault, he started it — with his stories — he made it worse — why couldn't you leave it alone? Stop staring at me!'

Fortune Teller
Mysterious clairvoyant

The Fortune Teller lives on the Chino-planet of Shan Shen. Her stall can be found in a run-down street market and it is there that she lures Donna into her room, promising to give a free reading because Donna has red hair. To help her predict the future, she asks Donna to tell her something of her past and Donna finds herself immediately transported back to a very real flashback of working at H.C. Clements. She forces Donna to rethink her past and take a different direction, creating a parallel world where Donna doesn't meet the Doctor and, as a result, he dies while fighting the Empress of the Racnoss. The Fortune Teller is amazed at Donna's strength to resist her and is scared of her, wondering what Donna will become. It is possible that she is working for the Trickster along with the Time Beetle.

Statistics

DEBUT	*Turn Left* (2008)
PLAYED BY	Chipo Chung
HOME	Shan Shen
STATUS	Enemy helper
HEIGHT	1.68m
SCARE RATING	[7] Don't speak to her
SPECIAL FEATURES	[7] Can let you know your future
WEAPONS	[8] The Time Beetle
LIKES	Predicting what will happen to you, chaos
DISLIKES	Donna Noble
TALK	'Make the choice again, Donna Noble, and change your mind, turn right!'

Time Beetle
Interfering insect

The Time Beetle is a large insect creature that feeds off time by manipulating it. It changes a life in a small way – meaning that people don't meet, children aren't born, and lives are completely different – but usually the universe fits in around it. However, with Donna, it created a huge new parallel world around her. The Time Beetle is part of the Trickster's Brigade, and the Fortune Teller helped it by getting it onto Donna's back. Once on her back it exists in a state of flux, which means that no one can touch it, and it is invisible to most humans. Donna becomes aware that certain people stare at her back for no reason – and is worried because there is nothing there. Rose Tyler uses technology from the TARDIS to show Donna what is living on her back. In the parallel world, Donna kills herself to save the universe and the Time Beetle dies.

Statistics

DEBUT	*Turn Left* (2008)
PLAYED BY	Not applicable
HOME	Unknown
STATUS	Enemy
HEIGHT	0.5m long
SCARE RATING	[8] Horrible
SPECIAL FEATURES	[8] Can change events
WEAPONS	[1] Not applicable
LIKES	Interfering with time
DISLIKES	Donna
TALK	'Hiss-tic-tic-tic.'

Rose Tyler

The Doctor's best friend

Rose Tyler meets the Doctor when he is trying to save Earth from the Nestene Consciousness and the Autons. After travelling with the Doctor for a long time, Rose becomes separated from him during a Dalek and Cyberman battle, and is left trapped in parallel universe with her mum and ex-boyfriend Mickey along with her parallel dad. When the Daleks attempt to destroy the universe, the stars start going out in her world. Working with UNIT in this other world, she attempts to find the Doctor again and she is able to get through into other worlds using a Dimension Canon – and is eventually able to help the Doctor fight back. The Doctor returns his friend to the parallel Earth with a human version of himself so they can live and grow old together. The Doctor thinks that Rose will be able to make the duplicate Doctor a better man.

Statistics

DEBUT	Rose (2005)
PLAYED BY	Billie Piper
HOME	Parallel Earth
STATUS	Best friend
HEIGHT	1.65m
SCARE RATING	[1] Not applicable
SPECIAL FEATURES	[8] Great friend, loyal, would do anything for the Doctor
WEAPONS	[5] A great big Dalek-destroying blaster
LIKES	The Doctor, danger, defending the planet
DISLIKES	The parallel world
TALK	'I spent all that time, trying to get away from this place. So I could find you. I'm not going back now.'

Captain Jack Harkness
Immortal Time Agent

Captain Jack Harkness
Immortal Time Agent

Captain Jack Harkness comes
from the 51st century. He meets
the Doctor and Rose for the first
time while he is working as a Time
Agent in the 1940s during the
Second World War. He travels
with the Doctor and Rose until he
is exterminated by the Daleks, but
Rose brings him back to life while
she has the powers of the Time
Vortex running through her head.
Unfortunately for Jack this means
that he can never die and will live
forever. He is currently running
Torchwood in Cardiff, protecting the
planet from alien menaces. When the
Daleks invade Earth, Harriet Jones
contacts Jack while she attempts
to track down the Doctor. He gets
aboard the Crucible to help the
Doctor and his friends fight back at
Davros and the Daleks. The Doctor
thinks Jack may, in the far future,
become the Face of Boe.

Statistics

DEBUT	*The Empty Child* (2005)
PLAYED BY	John Barrowman
HOME	Originally from the Boeshane Peninsula, now lives in Cardiff, Wales
STATUS	Friend
HEIGHT	1.85m
SCARE RATING	[2] Can be aggressive
SPECIAL FEATURES	[9] Access to alien tech, can live forever
WEAPONS	[5] Sonic blaster
LIKES	Flirting
DISLIKES	Alien invasions
TALK	'There's nothing I can do. I'm sorry. We're dead.'

Sarah Jane Smith
Journalist and defender of Earth

Sarah Jane Smith meets the Doctor when she is investigating a story for a newspaper about missing scientists. She is pretending to be her aunt at the time. She sneaks into the TARDIS by accident – and is transported back to the Middle Ages! Sarah Jane travels with the Doctor for some time, and they become great friends. The Doctor is forced to take her back home when the Time Lords ask him to return to Gallifrey, long before it is destroyed in the Time War. When she meets the Doctor years later, she tells him that the TARDIS had dropped her off in Aberdeen, and not her home in South Croydon. Sarah Jane now lives in Ealing with her adopted son Luke Smith. Along with a computer called Mr Smith, Sarah continues to work as a journalist, and helps save the planet from dangerous invasions, including attacks from the Daleks, Slitheen and the Sontarans.

Statistics

MODERN DEBUT	*School Reunion* (2006)
PLAYED BY	Elisabeth Sladen
HOME	London, England
STATUS	Friend
HEIGHT	1.63m
SCARE RATING	[1] Not applicable
SPECIAL FEATURES	[7] Good journalist
WEAPONS	[1] Not applicable – Sarah doesn't believe in them
LIKES	Her son Luke, K-9, the Doctor
DISLIKES	Weapons, blowing things up
TALK	'You act like such a lonely man. But look at you. You've got the biggest family on Earth!'

Luke Smith
Sarah Jane's son

Luke Smith is created from thousands of different human DNA samples by aliens called the Bane. They call him the archetype and plan to use him for various tests – and as a result, he is incredibly clever, and possesses a fantastic memory with the ability to absorb vast amounts of information very quickly. After defeating the Bane, Sarah Jane Smith adopts the boy and she gives him the name Luke. Sarah Jane is incredibly proud of her son and loves him very much. He starts at the local school along with his neighbour Maria and they both become friends with a boy called Clyde. Together with Sarah Jane, they encounter many strange and dangerous things. Perhaps the most dangerous is the Dalek invasion of Earth. The Doctor contacts Luke from the TARDIS and gets him to help return the planet to its correct place in time and space with Mr Smith.

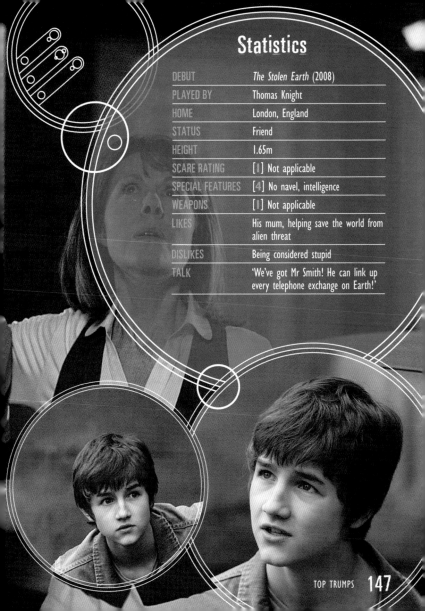

Statistics

DEBUT	*The Stolen Earth* (2008)
PLAYED BY	Thomas Knight
HOME	London, England
STATUS	Friend
HEIGHT	1.65m
SCARE RATING	[1] Not applicable
SPECIAL FEATURES	[4] No navel, intelligence
WEAPONS	[1] Not applicable
LIKES	His mum, helping save the world from alien threat
DISLIKES	Being considered stupid
TALK	'We've got Mr Smith! He can link up every telephone exchange on Earth!'

The Shadow Proclamation is an intergalactic police force based on a huge asteroid in space. The Doctor says they are just a posh name for outer space police, and they exist to enforce Galactic Law. The Shadow Proclamation uses the interplanetary police for hire known as the Judoon – and, like the Judoon, they are quick to pass judgement and make important decisions concerning crimes. When Earth disappears, the Doctor and Donna head to the Shadow Proclamation to see if they can help. They discover that 27 planets in total have been taken out of time and space. The Shadow Proclamation is led by the Shadow Architect, who looks quite sinister with red eyes and white hair, dressed in long black robes. According to the Strictures of the Shadow Proclamation, the Shadow Architect wants to seize the Doctor's TARDIS and use the Doctor to lead a war right across the universe – but the Doctor escapes before she does so.

Statistics

DEBUG	*The Stolen Earth* (2008)
PLAYED BY	Kelly Hunter (Shadow Architect) and Amy Beth Hayes (Albino Servant)
HOME	The Shadow Proclamation asteroid
STATUS	Friends
HEIGHT	Various
SCARE RATING	[4] Sinister stares
SPECIAL FEATURES	[3] Red eyes and slightly psychic
WEAPONS	[1] Not applicable, but the power of the Galactic Law
LIKES	Rules
DISLIKES	Disobedience
TALK	'Doctor! Come back! By the Holy Writ of the Shadow Proclamation, I order you to stop!'

Torchwood
Secret organisation

Torchwood
Secret organisation

Torchwood deals with all things alien.
In 1879, Queen Victoria sets up the
Torchwood Institute in Scotland after
an alien Werewolf attack. The Queen
wants to protect the country from
similar invasions and even the Doctor.
Over the years, Torchwood grows
into a big organisation, operating
from several locations, including
Torchwood Tower in London and a
base under Cardiff near a Rift in time
and space. Yvonne Hartman runs
the London Torchwood until she is
upgraded to a Cyberman during a
Dalek and Cyberman invasion. Nearly
800 Torchwood employees die or
go missing during the battle, and
eventually members of the Cardiff
Torchwood salvage pieces of alien
technology from the Torchwood
Tower ruins. Captain Jack Harkness
now leads a small group in Cardiff
along with Gwen Cooper and Ianto
Jones. Jack asks for Martha Jones'
help and she briefly joins the
team in Cardiff.

Statistics

DEBUT	*Tooth and Claw (2006)*
PLAYED BY	John Barrowman (Captain Jack Harkness), Eve Myles (Gwen Cooper), Burn Gorman (Dr. Owen Harper), Naoko Mori (Toshiko Sati), and Gareth David-Lloyd (Ianto Jones)
HOME	Cardiff, Wales
STATUS	Secret organisation
HEIGHT	Various
SCARE RATING	[1] Not applicable
SPECIAL FEATURES	[7] Gathering alien technology
WEAPONS	[8] The Rift in Cardiff
LIKES	Defending Earth
DISLIKES	Alien threats
TALK	Captain Jack Harkness: 'The 21st century is when it all changes.'

Dalek Caan

Mad Dalek

Dalek Caan is one of the four members of the Cult of Skaro, created by the Emperor to think up new ways of defeating Dalek enemies. After the Time War, he hides in the Void with the rest of the Cult along with the Genesis Ark, which contains millions of Daleks. The Cult escapes the battle of Carary Wharf using a Temporal Emergency Shift to 1930s New York, where their leader, Dalek Sec, merges with a human to save the Dalek race. When this doesn't work, Caan becomes the last surviving Dalek. He travels back in time to rescue Davros from the Time War. Travelling into the Time Vortex, Caan sees all the terrible results of Dalek destruction and is severely damaged and becomes mad. Dalek Caan manipulates the Time Lines so that Donna and the Doctor meet. He knows that eventually Donna will help bring about the destruction of the Davros and the Dalek race.

Statistics

DEBUT	*Army of Ghosts* (2006)
PLAYED BY	Voiced by Nicholas Briggs
HOME	Skaro
STATUS	Enemy
HEIGHT	1.80m
SCARE RATING	[9] Terrifying
SPECIAL FEATURES	[9] Can see the future, can manipulate the Time Lines
WEAPONS	[9] Dalek power
LIKES	Helping rid the universe of Dalek life
DISLIKES	Daleks
TALK	'I saw the Daleks, what we have done throughout Time and Space. I saw the truth of us, Creator, and I decreed: no more'

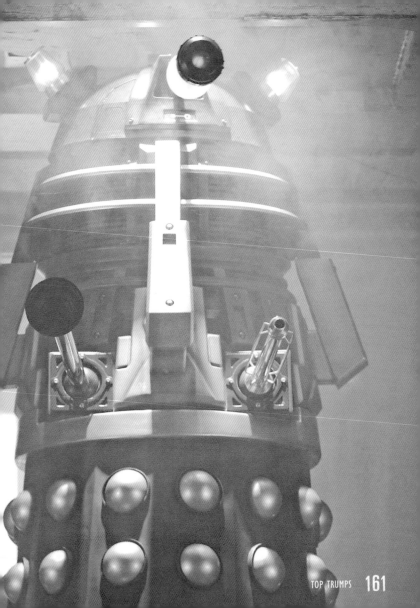

Supreme Dalek
Dangerous Dalek

The powerful and ruthless Supreme Dalek is the leader of the New Dalek Empire. Bright red, with three lights on his dome, and extra parts on this casing, the Supreme Dalek looks different from other Daleks in the empire. The Supreme Dalek plans to destroy everything in the universe with a Reality Bomb, leaving only Dalek life behind. Although he is created from cells in Davros' body, the Supreme Dalek keeps his creator in the dark vaults of the main Dalek spaceship and shows little respect for the scientist. He also thinks that Dalek Caan is an abomination, even though Caan is the reason that the Dalek race survives. When Donna stops the Reality Bomb, the Supreme Dalek descends to the vaults to exterminate everyone in it including Davros, but Captain Jack blows him up with his Defabricator Gun before he gets a chance to.

Statistics

MODERN DEBUT	*The Stolen Earth* (2008)
PLAYED BY	Voiced by Nicholas Briggs
HOME	The Crucible
STATUS	Dangerous enemy leader
HEIGHT	1.90m
SCARE RATING	[10] Completely terrifying
SPECIAL FEATURES	[9] Can fly, three lights on dome
WEAPONS	[10] Blaster, the Reality Bomb
LIKES	Dalek life, exterminating
DISLIKES	Dalek Caan, Davros, the Doctor
TALK	'Behold, Doctor! Behold the might of the true Dalek race!'

Davros
Dalek creator

Davros is the creator of the Daleks, a genius scientist who turns mutated creatures into the most powerful race in the universe. The Doctor meets Davros for the first time when the Time Lords send him back in time to the creation of the horrific Daleks. The Dalek creatures turn against their creator – after all, he isn't pure Dalek life like them so must be exterminated. Davros has been stopped several times, but has been rescued by his creations. The Doctor thinks that Davros is dead, because he sees the Dalek command ship fly into the jaws of the Nightmare Child, at the Gates of Elysium, in the very first year of the Time War. Dalek Caan flies into the Time War and rescues Davros, who then uses cells from the his own body to build a new Dalek Empire. In spite of this, the Daleks treat him badly and keep him locked away on the Crucible.

Statistics

MODERN DEBUT	*The Stolen Earth* (2008)
PLAYED BY	Julian Bleach
HOME	Skaro
STATUS	Enemy
HEIGHT	1.78m
SCARE RATING	[10] Horrific
SPECIAL FEATURES	[10] One single metal hand, base like a Dalek
WEAPONS	[10] The Daleks, the Reality Bomb
LIKES	Daleks
DISLIKES	The Doctor
TALK	'Nothing can stop the detonation, Doctor. Nothing and no one!'

Judoon

Police for hire

Judoon
Police for hire

The Judoon are a race of hulking creatures that work as hired police for whoever wants to pay the most. They look very fierce – the massive Judoon head has two horns between a set of emotionless eyes. The Judoon space police dress in leather combat gear – big leather boots, thick leather skirt and a massive black helmet for protection. To help communicate they are able to adopt alien languages by scanning sounds, assimilating them and plugging the scanning device into a nozzle on their chest. The Judoon use an H_2O scoop to remove a hospital from planet Earth and drop it on the Moon. According to Galactic Law the Judoon have no jurisdiction over Earth, so they need to isolate the hospital in order to capture the Plasmavore who is hiding there. When the Doctor and Donna arrive at the Shadow Proclamation, they meet a patrol of Judoon that work there.

Statistics

DEBUT	*Smith and Jones* (2007)
PLAYED BY	Various. Judoon Captain played by Paul Kasey. Voiced by Nicholas Briggs
HOME	Unknown
STATUS	Unintelligent thugs
HEIGHT	2m
SCARE RATING	[8] Scary
SPECIAL FEATURES	[7] Thick battle armour, language and species scanner
WEAPONS	[8] Blaster
LIKES	Stomping, justice, cataloguing
DISLIKES	Physical assault
TALK	'Sco! Bo Tro! No! Flo! Jo! Ko! Fo! To! Do!'

K-9
Robot dog

K-9 is a highly intelligent robot dog.
There are four versions of the robot
– three of which are built by the
Doctor. The Time Lord meets the
original K-9 in the year 5000AD. This
K-9 travels with the Doctor until
the robot decides to stay with the
Doctor's friend Leela. The Doctor
then builds a second model, which
helps him find the Key to Time.
After many adventures, this model is
damaged by Time Winds and has to
leave the TARDIS. A third model is
given to Sarah Jane Smith on Earth
– a present from the Doctor so the
robot can look after his old friend.
This model is blown up while fighting
the Krillitane, so the Doctor builds a
fourth K-9 for Sarah Jane to replace
him. This K-9 sends the TARDIS
base codes to Mr Smith so that the
TARDIS can drag Earth back to its
correct time and place after the
Dalek invasion.

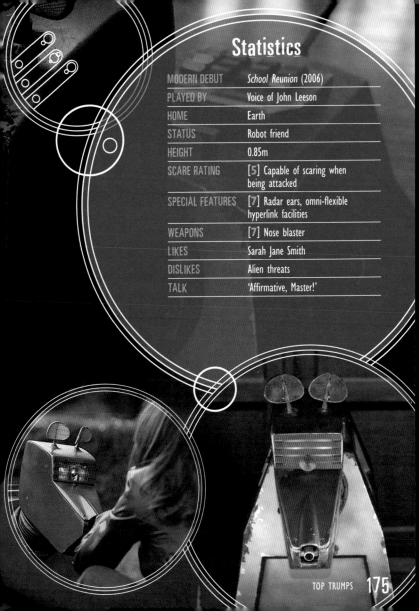

Statistics

MODERN DEBUT	*School Reunion* (2006)
PLAYED BY	Voice of John Leeson
HOME	Earth
STATUS	Robot friend
HEIGHT	0.85m
SCARE RATING	[5] Capable of scaring when being attacked
SPECIAL FEATURES	[7] Radar ears, omni-flexible hyperlink facilities
WEAPONS	[7] Nose blaster
LIKES	Sarah Jane Smith
DISLIKES	Alien threats
TALK	'Affirmative, Master!'

Mickey Smith

Rose's old boyfriend

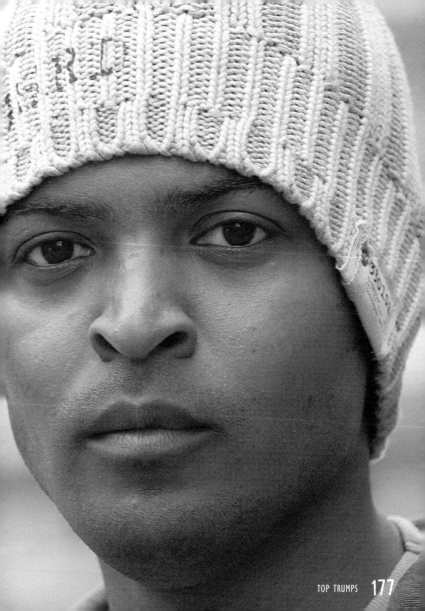

Mickey Smith
Rose's old boyfriend

Mickey Smith doesn't start off as the bravest of the Doctor's friends, but he goes on to become a defender of the Earth! Mickey is left behind when Rose goes off travelling in the TARDIS with the Doctor. At first, he hates the Time Lord for taking his girlfriend away – even though the Doctor asks him if he would like to travel with them. After battling with the Krillitane at Deffry Vale school and meeting another friend of the Doctor's – Sarah Jane Smith – Mickey decides he wants to see what he is missing and joins them. He isn't travelling for very long before he decides to stay behind in a parallel universe, where he helps defeat the Cybermen. He is later joined by Rose and Jackie until a huge Dalek invasion breaks down the walls between the parallel worlds. When Mickey comes back through to his original Earth to help defeat the Daleks he eventually decides to remain there.

Statistics

DEBUT	*Rose* (2005)
PLAYED BY	Noel Clarke
HOME	London, England
STATUS	Friend
HEIGHT	1.75m
SCARE RATING	[1] Not applicable
SPECIAL FEATURES	[4] Good with computers
WEAPONS	[5] Big Dalek-destroying blaster
LIKES	Defending Earth
DISLIKES	Being left behind
TALK	'There's nothing left for me there, now. Certainly not Rose.'

Jackie Tyler

Rose's mum

Jackie Tyler
Rose's mum

Jackie Tyler is Rose's mum and, like Rose, her life changed when the Doctor appeared. When her daughter vanishes, Jackie spends twelve months searching for her and blames Rose's old boyfriend Mickey for her disappearance. Jackie makes Mickey's life miserable during that time – but they later become good friends again. When Rose reappears she the blames Doctor for stealing her away. When she discovers travels in the TARDIS she makes the Doctor promise that he will look after her, a promise he always keeps. She lives with a parallel version of her husband Pete on a parallel Earth, and they have a son called Tony. She comes back to her original Earth with Mickey to fight the Daleks. The Daleks capture Jackie and she almost becomes a victim of a Reality Bomb test, but teleports to safety with seconds to spare. The Doctor returns her to the parallel Earth after defeating the Daleks.

Statistics

DEBUT	*Rose* (2005)
PLAYED BY	Camille Coduri
HOME	London, England, Parallel Earth
STATUS	Friend
HEIGHT	1.65m
SCARE RATING	[1] Not applicable unless she's angry
SPECIAL FEATURES	[2] Good at making tea in a crisis
WEAPONS	[5] Big Dalek-destroying blaster
LIKES	Rose, Pete
DISLIKES	Monsters
TALK	'What d'you mean? The Doctor's taking us back home, isn't he?'

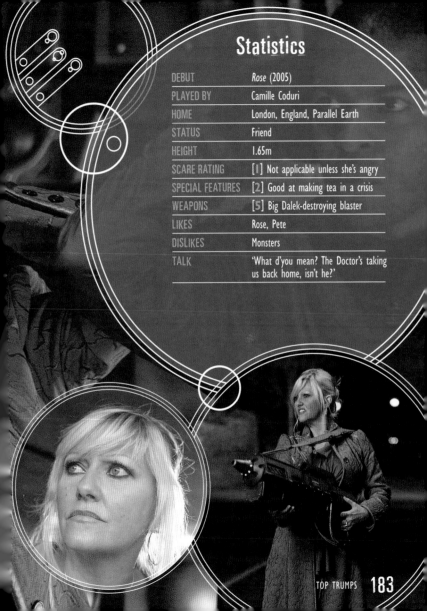

Harriet Jones
Former Prime Minster

Harriet Jones is the Member of
Parliament for Flydale North when
she meets the Doctor. She becomes
the new Prime Minister and has
to defend Earth when the Sycorax
invade. In place of the Queen's
speech, Harriet puts out a plea on
Christmas Day for the Doctor to
help them. When the Sycorax leave
Earth she gives the order for their
massive spaceship to be destroyed.
This act angers the Doctor and he
loses all faith he has in Harriet Jones.
Later, Harriet develops the Subwave
Network, a sentient piece of
software that is programmed to seek
out anyone and everyone who can
help contact the Doctor. She knows
that one day Earth will be in danger
and the Doctor will be needed.
Harriet helps Jack, Martha and Sarah
Jane locate the TARDIS, but the
Daleks find her and exterminate her.
On the parallel Earth, Harriet Jones
is the President of Great Britain.

Statistics

DEBUT	*Aliens of London* (2005)
PLAYED BY	Penelope Wilton
HOME	London, England
STATUS	Friend
HEIGHT	1.70m
SCARE RATING	[1] Not applicable
SPECIAL FEATURES	[5] The Subwave Network
WEAPONS	[5] Uses Torchwood to destroy the Sycorax
LIKES	Being fair, the Doctor
DISLIKES	Alien threats
TALK	'Harriet Jones, former Prime Minister....'

 3 The Colour of Darkness
OUT FEBRUARY!

 4 The Depths of Despair
OUT MARCH!

5 The Vampire of Paris
OUT APRIL!

6 The Game of Death
OUT MAY!

COVERS NOT FINAL

7 The Planet of Oblivion
OUT JUNE!

8 The Picture of Emptiness
OUT JULY!

9 The Art of War
OUT AUGUST!

10 The End of Time
OUT SEPTEMBER!

'Collected' Party

Sign up at www.darksmithlegacy.com, complete the quest online or send in the receipts for two of the books, and you could find yourself at an exclusive party at the end of the Darksmith Legacy series to be held at a secret location with the chance to win lots of Doctor Who prizes and collectables.

o order ring Customer Services on 0870 607 7600.
n www.penguin.com
r on www.darksmithlegacy.com

www.haynes.co.uk